GranDogma

for

Sacred Village Earth

Be-Loved Affirmations Inspired by
Planet Storytellers News®

Cynthia Kay Castle

BALBOA
PRESS

A DIVISION OF HAY HOUSE

Balboa Press books may be ordered through booksellers or by contacting:

Balboa Press
A Division of Hay House
1663 Liberty Drive
Bloomington, IN 47403
www.balboapress.com
1 (877) 407-4847

Print information available on the last page.

ISBN: 978-1-9822-0745-8 (sc)
ISBN: 978-1-9822-0746-5 (e)

Balboa Press rev. date: 07/12/2018

CONTENTS

DEDICATIONS

Edgar Loyd (Skip) Castle, Jr.
1954-2006
"I Am Not the First"

"I am not the first, nor the last to ever have loved you so;
For if the first and last have come and gone,
the best you may never know."

Visionary poem written in 1972 by Skip, a peaceful beautiful father of Ashley Bree and Zerin Thomas Castle. He was a Coyote teacher partner for almost thirty years in this physical dimension. Song Dog poet was a beautiful trickster who first opened my heart to trust love and shared a dimensional dance for thirty years. His story could be a movie from his Lubbock Symphony rhythms as a bass, viola, cello and "sort a" violin player on Saturday night. His Sunday at his mothers' behest was at church but in defiance at the Methodist versus non-dancing Baptist Uncle's. The tragic quadriplegic loss of his musical mentor Ben of 'Street Theatre' prompted a powerful healing by his Shaman. His Comanche traditions foretold he would marry a blue-eyed Cindy but that his life would end tragically between the graduation of his son and daughter. With his difficult life he strove the courageous use of snake medicine who's tales end in a peaceful transition to the Beyond - Beyond.

Beauty of Heart

Beauty of heart and mind
Gift of joy from God to mankind

Precious light being know strength
In love surrounding ewe life's length

Angels sing when you smile
And laugh in triumph each mile

Release past fears and tears
Open room for joy my dear

Be protected from heaven to Earth's fire core
Leave fear and sadness as your guardian angel's chore

Thank ewe to Julie Anne and Laura Ann whom I originally wrote this affirmation. My beautiful heart sisters who listened with care and knew me when I didn't recognize myself early in my traumatic brain injury crazy "who am I phase" because of the daily status migrainosus for over four years.

Heart Hugs OF A
Golden Brown Eyed Girl

An orator who spoke open doors without license so bold
Mastered Be-love hugs, where brazen shields unfold

Flames of laughter blazed opened guarded paths
To warm hearts with golden-brown eyes that end wrath

Blessed clear essence with her gift of presence
Docent smile lights the room where regrets end

Knows eternal truth to illumine false hope
Loosen ties that entangle dependent ropes

Welcomes dynamic notes that balance truth
Resonant heart vibrations; end deceit rouse

Clears each day with deep breath to know golden light
Awaken gifts that fuels loving creative sight

Dedicated to my daughter Ashley Bree
Born free to Be love
With her Golden Heart Hugs

Ashley-Bree originally with a hyphen-declined by her Father still has it's meaning as the nurturing strength humane being with the loving resilience of a tree who exchanges cleansing breath. Bree means born free to be love unconditional.

Johnny and Ashley Bree
"Truth in Blue Eyes"

He met her on a summer's ocean wave
Eyes of blue truth taught her how to be brave

She sparkled at his creative wisdom
Angst left her breath to awaken freedom

They cared before known it safe to be free
Two hearts grew as one, as Duke whined lonely

Her loyal heart distracted her moments
From his faithful blue eyes love so intense

His beam focused on waves that brought her near
Their hearts opened fully invest so dear

The family grown with friend and a home
Building bridges that linked roads fun to roam.

Castle-Carpenter Merger
Married 2015

Golden Heart Hugs
Zerin Thomas

Zerin bringer of the hearts of gold, it's been told
Mastered be-love hugs, that heal hurts so cold

Flames of laughter blazed opened shielded paths
To warm sweet hearts, his blue-eyed view ends wrath

His conception reverberant of Buddhas' laughter
As lotus heart blossomed truth ending disasters

His gift of presence clears be-loves' essence
His docent smile lights rooms where regrets end

Eternal truth's sound illumines false hope
Loosens ties that entangle dependent ropes

Welcomes dynamic notes that balance truth
Resonant vibrations; end deceit's rouse

Clears each day with deep breath to know gold light
Awakens gifts that fuel creative sight

Zerin, my son whose name in Pakistan means bringer of gold, shares a uniquely wonderful ability as his sister of being a healing hugger. His life partner Shawna is a wonderful hugger, a blessing to our family. Zerin chose her wisely as both are amazing unconditionally loving. My first two weeks after my car accident I was floating in between worlds on my son's couch as I unconsciously spoke to everyone entering the apartment. Apparently entertainingly but that's a bit of a longer story. There will be some other references that are part of another book entitled 'Biohackers' in editing that unravels the return of retrograde memory swirls from 1972 to 2015. The Vortex void memories returned in lightning flashes to illuminate my path; highlighted from the dark void in 'Rabbit Vortex' awakening memories in a healing paradigm.

CHAPTER 1

Awaking Retrograde Memory Loss Through Poetry

- A bit of the trauma drama intersection near death view port.

- The Functioning Nurse brain that recreated the map back to heart and mind balance through the familiar to become a being in love able to trust love again

- Souls Merge to Love Freely

- "The merging of minds aligned with heart engages a connective human experience that can heal a traumatized mind. The energetic merging can stimulate an experience that goes beyond empathy and compatibility. Be in enjoyment of the beautiful alignment of souls in partnering projects to reduce feelings of separation. Merge with your whole self to expand awareness into a multidimensional world where two gathered become a universe of possibilities. Soul merge in discernment with the one who brings infinity to love freely." Cynthia Kay Castle November 9, 2014

The addendum to this original post today cautions that in traumatic brain injury, any enmeshment relationships can imbalance and further impair the relationship to self. My nurse "hippie-me" viewpoint brought people into our home when I sensed a wounded soul. In my initial healing phase, I did not remember who I was as an adult my appropriate age. The need to help others when you do not want to face your own care needs caused enmeshment in grief recovery from my late husband's long terminal illness and death. I would relate to anyone interesting that understood a part of my fractured memories, or bereavement to bolster my constructs as a professional. At the time I wrote this I did not have a care plan team but received medical treatment with caring faces in multiple emergency room visits. The memories are in flash moment recaps that return with lightning flash synesthesia migraines which were part of my brains attempt to recallibrate to whole-self.

When experiencing a union beyond compare and not explainable to anyone you know after accident, illness or traumatic separation of self-identity; seek immediate medical attention. This can be signs of an enmeshment relationship with someone who may be unable to heal themselves and may devalue or misalignment values that were part of your grounded self. If you have already as a loved one or someone concerned for a loved one ruled out physiological, psychological pathologies by a physician, there may be concern of cultish influences or drug cultural peers in play.

Palliative Medical-Spiritual Caring: For Memory Hospice celebration of life and recovering quality memory function after trauma. A nightmare that replayed during my brain injury recovery that began five years after my late husband's death was that our deaths were one in the same; his physical and mine the death of who I had been as a hospice nurse. This paradigm can occur with depression after loss and for some leads to suicidal ideation with the inability to reconcile the loss or your imperfection self during a slow death over seven years.

Awakening Retrograde Memory Loss Through Dream Journaling & Poetry

What I saw and heard in my out of body near death experience in 2012 I was the conscious observer hovering over my eight-year old self talking to a light. Entranced by the rapid hand movement of two crooked dark varnish sticks I appeared to be telling a story to a shrouded glowing figure. In my favorite outfit made by my mother of bright seersucker yellow I spoke in wooden rhythms as if a song were being made. Suddenly I was aware of the other option-me crumpled up on the side of the embankment, the light-me flashed into the moving vehicle. I heard myself inspire the longest breath as my folded body raised off my lap. I sprung to life to grab the steering wheel to bring the car away from the wire guard railing.

The driver had apparently been struck by the broken glass of the metal brackets and knocked for a loop as his hands seemed to reach toward heaven. The rhythmic sound of the metal straps counted the milliseconds before another crash. I struggled to slow the car as I straddled to put my leg over his to stop the car just inches before the construction warning sign. I woke up in the passenger's seat with a memory of the fifties style highway patrolman making sure we were okay at the back of our car in his brown uniform and odd Canadian Mounty looking hat. Something familiar of his face shown in the light that started to come to me as a dream messenger as the "friend" of the officers who picked up twelve-year old run-away me from Youth City all those years ago.

I tried to shake off the feeling of knowing but the dated fifties dress uniform began to dawn as a knowing thought technically impossible. As I used an oriental medicine Tuina technique for nausea on myself the left and right brain collation realized his identity. The memory resurfaced in flash that the first teacher of Asian body therapy Tuina had been my highway patrol childhood heroes' wife. I had pronounced his death over two decades prior as his hospice nurse; barely mesmerized by the coincidence of him being one of those highway patrol saints. I began to remember his counsels on our long journey back to the fostered orphans home as a spiritual man whose physical presence would assist me on a detoured stretch of highway to bring another real-life awakening; this life is not over yet.

What dawned on me was the multidimensional void of time constraints the universe operated in bring people together in need. Something warm came over me as I realized that the light I was "speaking" to with my wooden language tools had become that sweet protector I had met again through the magnificence of quantum beingness in our limitless connections in love. The memories of his wife's Amish wood stove cornbread and stories of wisdom loomed as a guidepost of the future that was to unfold as new me.

I began to filter life-long "click memories" in my gray matter as she was not the first one to teach me an oriental technique described in her simple woman ways. The reality of a simple tool of hers for nausea became inexplicably more important as a teacher who like Don Bacon was meant to be in my life for over thirty years as well. Then the third dimensional days of hard reality of dependent terror dawned. I watched people who once showed love began to fear the permanent disability view me. I tried to remain focused to reflect on the grace of life that I had been given to hardly notice their frightened compassionate eyes of the new unrecognizable me.

Within a year the stress of my daily migraines impaired working ability, the mental violence became the cliché that I never thought I would face. The few night shift hours I managed to work alerted the seasoned caring nurses that nonverbal ways were a disconcerting social introverted changed self. I somehow blocked out the apparently episodic violence as related to the financial burdens until I left nursing. I finally left all my possessions to seek refuge with my family after a warning dream of violent death came from Grandma blue eyes.

The retrograde memory loss of a lifetime of social details began three days after the accident. The curious thing about brains and internship or triage on call training is that its' information storage is apparently housed somewhere outside our fragile gray matter. Though on some days I prayed for the confusing dreams and nightmares to subside in trade for loss of all that unusable knowledge. Now I am grateful for the use in understanding compassion for others in brain injury or post traumatic amygdala flight or fight reactions to our mundane routines. Though I knew I could not trade one for the other, the love of my family never let me give up on the annoying over burden of knowledge that was no longer reasonable or prudent for clinical oversight management.

The sorrow seemed to be diverted by the memories returning in lightning flashes of synesthesia technicolor sounds and smells that would shake my once confident self over the next four years.

The precision clarity of the detailed timeline mixed with almost psychedelic migraine storms started to re-collate the missteps that lead to a path in need of correction and acceptance of the loss of my thirty-year marriage partner. But what I now missed a decade since my late husbands' loss was the confident me. I remembered that sweet wife of my hospice highway patrol hero or angel in disguise had reminded me that even a grandmother can know a little about oriental medicine and still make cornbread a good story back drop.

I began this past year with a new integrated spiritual medical care team who helped to give me the courage to right down the words to help others understand the introverted post trauma brain. The inexplicable that initially could not speak the words to those closest to their hearts, began to write the living Great Mystery God of the quantum. A larger than my whiny universe kept sending messages to connect the hearts understanding as I wrote in my gold notebook a poetry path of strengths to bring back to course a life with meaning to be love unconditional.

Through Quantum Zenergetics techniques, prayer and my spiritual medical care team, I am rebuilding the dendrite links in the brain to awaken the retrograde amnesia loss I experienced. I studied several psychiatric and spiritual models healing in traumatic memory, but the one I loved most was Stephen Hawking's 'Free Radical Paradigm'. I realized that retrograde memory recovery was like a spiritual hospice quality life honor review of a person's end of life transition that could be recreated in Stephen Hawking's Free Radical Paradigm'. The latest psychological model I studied is aptly named radical acceptance. I first heard the term from 'Hand of God' a series created by Ben Walkins that aired on video streaming a couple of years ago. Though initially; it was my least favorite, I began to realize that accepting the unpleasant memories were the keys to unlock repressed ones and became radically more help than I initially realized. For example, the merging of Carl Jung, Sigmund Freud, and Gestalt psychology theories ever present in my mind began the conscious and unconscious fusion of events. The wormholes in my timeline began to emerge as recovered memory rerouted through the subconscious dream or lucid states.

Spiritual wellness theoretically begets wholeness; it is important to identify patient religious or ritualized practices significant to current day practice evolution. My favorite part of psychological dreamscape derived from my love of American Indian spiritualism and Carl Jung synchronicity theories seems to merge dreams with Gestalt psychology. (1.,2.) It comes as no surprise that the term spiritual eclectic birthed of spiritual philosophers, who love the study of ritualized religious practices on display through behavioral, social sciences. The Gestalt method as defined in the Merriam-Webster dictionary seems to exemplify a trajectory that may have begun from child repressed traumas initiating a compartmentalized coping mechanism.

Gestalt Psychology, "the study of perception and behavior from the standpoint of an individual's response to configurational wholes with stress on the uniformity of psychological and physiological events and rejection of analysis into discrete events of stimulus, perception, and response." (2. Quote from Merriam-Webster)

As an eclectic spiritual philosopher, I started learning as a child from a strict subservient version of females in the Pentecostal church fostered by my father. The miraculous healing that I witnessed numerous times through adulthood gave respect for traditions but drove me to medical sciences for greater understanding of quantum energetic techniques. The evangelical Catholic and Methodist Protestant churches, where I studied miracles also mirrored some beautiful technical separations. The behavioral science of group doctrine separations is quite an in-depth research within much non-Christian and Christian focus; to "insiders". The divisions may baffle necessity to perceived "outsiders" of church doctrines including the original divisions from Catholic, Southern Baptist to the Church of Latter Day Saints and the Church of Scientology. I studied my compiled life experience beliefs with the Course in Miracles, various Christian church memberships until I became a Universal Life Minister in 1999 and furthered the study of Tibetan Buddhism and Unity Church doctrine (3.). As a hospice nurse before the United States popularly separated hospice from home health in the 1990's, I was able to use all spiritual and medical teachings to help my patients.

Reconstructing the conscious memory loss from dream both recurrent and symbolic was the key that unlocked memories that spanned a lifetime of repressed trauma to strengthen the child's heart ability to love the unlovable in myself and others. To achieve a timeline from a less emotional state, I utilized a spiritual, medical hospice care plan model. The hospice care plan combines every aspect of spirituality and cultural, medical heritage issues significant to a terminal patient. In my case, terminality was the fluctuating stages of consciousness after traumatic brain injuries like a waking coma. A combination of Tibetan Buddhism Reiki healing techniques, Freudian, Jungian, eclectic-spirituality, Allopathic Hospice care planning and Zen Shiatsu Chinese medicine theory inspirations came together for my personalized care plan now known as Quantum Zenergetics Ask-ewe Solutions.

Perhaps to the outsider not understanding the personal life story of me, might see the customized care plan as unique choices of rituals honored as a spiritual eclectic. But what I learned in hospice care planning is that religion and medicine commingled. The socialized rituals from my youth memory comforts included multiple family definition changes. My security and deep love of my Great Grandparents rearing me until age five helped uncomplicate young parents that became a tumultuous foster group campus that commingled with retrograde memory voids. The near-death transitions to semi-wakeful post-concussive status, brought back many repressed memories before the adult retrograde lost ones resurfaced.

The repressed traumatic memories from childhood were locked away in a compartmental defense field and helped explain unexpected allegiance to anchors outside of my children's understanding. Transference helps explain how a caregiver can be a recipient of trust to protect children from painful memories. The compounding trust transference issue also occurred after my husband's death. The person of transference may be completely unexpectedly or unknown to family members. Life transition anchor members that the family may not know; often say to hospice workers, "I just knew I had to be here this evening." As a hospice nurse, I cared for a resentful family after a twenty-year-old romance focus of their mothers was a surprise living will confidant designee, who became a great comfort during her end of life care. In coma status or near-death events, the people we love may be those we want to protect from the knowledge we feel may impair relationships or be shockingly graphic. In the case of violent rape or the atrocities of the Holocaust, many parents give cryptic recounts to avoid the psychological scarring they felt might be passed on in the awareness seen in their children's eyes. The people we know who represent a stable trust or reference anchor help us to recapture the compassion of humanity and this life's meaning again. For many, this is not a person but a deity or religious, spiritual advisor.

The important legal thing to note as people become either more affluent or more politically significant is that the last rights or dying confessions designee may become a player in coma status clients as our brain computer interface technology improves. In my verbose state, I became obsessed with the amount of information that may become precious to someone in a coma state that desperately cannot speak to a trusted designee as the perpetrator may have been the cause of the coma. Many legal ramifications as a hospice nurse paralleled my frustrations in expressive communication aphasia. I drafted a document titled Sovereign Eagle Communication to acquaint a society to the potential complications of brain-computer interface technology used to investigate traumatic retrograde amnesia. (4.)

The privacy of near death versus death bed confessions may be difficult to measure as spiritual, while legal brain death is increasingly indeterminable due to innovative changes in technology. The singular purpose of the document was to improve living will designee privacy issues for citizens that value spiritual or medical treatments. The video recordings during experimental phases to save a life or identify identity may necessitate a living will short form including organ donor consistent with the driver's license or citizen identification. Tomorrow a living will designee or spiritual-medical communicator can be established by a brain-computer-interface with coma victims or someone near death transition. We serve our citizen rights to privacy in transition states as either social, spiritual, medical or spiritual-medical privacy. A homeless person or refugee may have an undiagnosed post-traumatic stress that may be described as a waking coma status with a social-emotional communication deficit.

In summary, the new technology savvy attorney will have the "vulnerable-life" living will document to include a social-cultural-spiritual-medical model emulated in end of life palliative hospice care. The brain-computer interface technologists are now creating the devices that will make this document integral to establish the end of life or life termination point definitions, that honor cultural or spiritual practices. This type of living will help someone to have a trust designee who honors choices that may have kept horrors or secrets. The vault of repressed memories or coveted secrets kept sacred may be the key that have kept psychological trauma reverberations real or imagined from being felt in the innocent eyes of their loved ones.

The first few poems may be difficult to hear of difficulties that nurses and some metaphysicians or spiritual leaders hear as returning memories of people I cared for mixed with early childhood and early marriage memories. To protect identities, I comingled co-worker or distant family stories. The interesting phenomenon is that the nursing school and career memories remained intact giving me a delusion of normalcy for a few months the first year after the passenger car accident, where I saw myself out of body.

When the difficulties of denying my late husbands', death began to dawn was after my son had an emergency appendectomy narrowly returning from Prague to begin an English teaching program. As most mothers know, the relationship with a son immolates the best things they wish for their own spiritual partnerships to aspire to. My daughter was the voice of wisdom in vocational decisions that merged with a love of mixing social and work relationships to bring the best of both worlds. My sons' surgery illuminated the fallacy of my denial, likely due to my poor parental skills after his father's death. But I did not recognize that I had no outside social life relationships less than a year before the domestic isolation and debilitating car accident occurred.

These poems will focus on some of the dreams of near loss of self, family or time periods in and out of conscious the first few weeks. The first few years after the 2012 car accident when the daily migraines resulted in out of body experiences to avoid pain, I began to plan an escape to family sanctuary in September of 2012. A recurrent story after trauma or loss of life is vulnerability for financial manipulation relationships. If your loved one in grief of partner loss or traumatic injury loss develops a relationship with one sided financial or emotional support systems, especially with increasing social isolation, please get help for your family or friend. In grief or trauma, a person's defense mechanisms are impaired many resorting to excessive dream sleep escape or being out of touch with reality. Let the details of the poems ring truth for your own story.

I wrote many in iambic pentameter. I hope the rhythm will assist your journey to awaken your own story as it allowed mine to travel with greater ease to the pages that began to inspire my own healing and awakening inspirational mentor teachings. The painting happened during the most difficult part of remembering that I was no long a professional self, but I felt a renewed love of Earth and her resources in a poem and painting entitled 'Timeless Ocean Healing'.

The 'Timeless Ocean' painting is of the needed healing waters of the rivers over our Earth to be cleansed through crystalline caves. The Colorado River tributaries that once fed seasonal creeks over greater areas of the Four Corners that nurtured land down to the southern American shores. The lower left corner depicts a sacred American Indian tribal area where wars were lost. With those losses, land became owned, thereby separating shared grazing rights honored by our ancestors.

Enchanted Rock is now a spiritual place for inspired sunsets of resonant truth granite. The upper right is a merger of the infinity and yin-yang symbols reflecting the choice for clear Earth waters. The lower right corner is the Texas Gulf shore, where the choice of free-flowing rivers bring rebirth to replenish our timeless ocean and bring optimal bird migration sanctuaries that feed our ocean.

Expanded Moment Between

The expanded moment at the transition awareness at soma death is a place where cosmic law consciousness becomes integral to dimensional choices of divine will creator. Recognition that dualistic paradigm Earth is a linear time playground that is operational under the illusion of separation from all life Creation. A place where budding awareness learns choice consequence. The moment placed in between where the operating system of the illusion of singularity knows the full inspiration of a limitless creators' paradigm disguised through a simple man's vision labeled Stephen Hawking.

The silence between the stars brighten awareness to those darkest of nights of the soul in transformation. In the heart open to the law of grace taught by Jesus Christ principles and the compassion of Siddhartha Buddha, each will know that the will of heavenly Creator is to thrive in eternal unconditional love known to many as The Great Mystery of God.

Be Love Now
Mitakuye Oyasin
Namaste'
Shalom
Amen

Bare Hope

Young mother of heart insight blooms new life
Red gold locks speak past incantations knife

Is this path paved by blood released in fear?
Forged inner strength outside she persevered

When does donor labels congeal stagnate?
Is the dolce of life possible from repugnant

Metal bar shadows revealed a hero
Justice came released at birth time zero

Time forgot how to love, though silence spoke
Unknown scares whole; through his birth she awoke

Who is she of strength to bare trust in love
For sweet heart beats new hope gentle as dove

Respond able heroes can be trauma nurses at the emergency room and maybe the ones to greet a new born unexpected as someone we could love. Sometimes the gathering of information in an unconditional manner helps us to hear another path opening from that trauma. They help bring a bundle of joy from someone we barely survived knowing. The nurses I met through the emergency room helped me to remember that surviving and breathing new life after trauma is the road to recovery, these heroes picked up the broken stories that begin a reset for a path off course. Nurses never share personal patient details; like priests they listen to confessionals and assist without judgement an overwhelmed life to empowerment. Occasionally they bring in a new life that was forged from a rape in prison and help someone hear love in a newborn's cry. 'Bare Hope' is a cumulative story about some nurses who helped me to learn that I deserved to be loved even as an innocent new born conceived in a traumatic way, we never expected to love.

Nurses We Know

They mend broken parts aching to belong
Alert alarms brings urgency to calm

Explaining optimum courses to treat
When ears hurt to hear, in fear of defeat

Stabilizing touch reconnects life rope
To family surrounding in loving hope

A nurse supports each family member
From Father to sister all hearts; tender

From paper care plans to healing with hugs
Diversity rarely seen with tired shrugs

The family who loves a nurse shares them
With pride grown stronger in tandem

Remembered
'Girl Talk'

This one of youth far more intelligent, never blind
Ruled the caverns where memory repressed the unkind

The unconscious observer began to crave her awakening
For things that happened; shivers under covers quaking

The soup of stories mixed with broth of lucid truth
Opened her mind to blind hate that called evil's sleuth

Messages quickly spoken, first only one or two
Sought stronger aid to investigate duality review

Unraveled hidden locks began to bring open house
Shared opened compartment to bring day and night rouse

She first emerged odd age from the nightmares repressed
I remembered her last night as champion solving evils confessed

Her other heart is mine, strong fearless oblivious to evil
Held her head's compartmentalized room's together - invasions civil

Her warrior cries of native tongue wronged need sound no more
Girl talk has flung open compartments once repressed by gore

Tools of the mind may be the resilience survived
Now hope awakened merged self, void relations contrived

Rabbit Vortex

Intersects of past and present futures
Swirls conscious choice of separation cures

Grounding understanding thrives delight
Brings purpose of self-lost in dark night

Divided lines romance with life's last breath
Earth's musk reveals star's recycling end quest

Life path corrections once near death's blank stare
Memory awakens void in fresh air

Time dilation - energy's light and sound
Rings pulsed heart beats rejoice in love now found

Choice opens love's arms to remove death's knife
Compassion for renewed self-brought me life

Behind swollen confusion contusion
Conscious aware released black delusion

Rabbit vortex darkness dawns recovered
Lost data reconciles path discovered

"Where Kaleidoscopic vision heals Rabbit Vortex"

References for my theories in this poem may be better understood from these sources.:

1. Program "Through the Wormhole" narrated by Morgan Freeman. Episode aired 05/10/2017 on the Science Channel. Great program that I am going to watch more of.

2. Pineal Gland DMT: http://www.trinfinity8.com/pineal-gland-dmt-a-pathway-to-psychic-abilities/

3. Zenergetic Transformations: Dream Vortexes and kaleidoscope healing paradigms https://sites.google.com/s/1bd7THAOIAhr6t3veh_GHTYi3qhST2nXa/p/0B5oRiZNy6Vn1TWpuZW5ZTzJEMm8/edit

4. Stephen Hawking's 'Free Radical Paradigm' a theoretical physicist view first theorized in 2008.

Compassionate Trust
Maps of Heart

Letting go to know myself though I never stole his secret map
The map that taught me to know compassion of self once more

Though I dreamt of him perhaps of many disguises of a beautiful self
He offered the ride just past the escape of hopeless lies trap of loss

A decade passed before I awoke to know the dream message
The message of choice to be or to leave life behind on that highway

With memories filled with blanks the left and right began to awaken
Then I saw his infinite self in my darkness, as it shone on my face

They saw a crutch; not to know what opened to heal trust
A shiny tool I once knew in another dimensional space

May only the new me awake from dream in way-showers wake
Released dependence began life of compassion for me as you wake

Thank you map of hearts to other dimensions of compassionate trust
Release Doubting Thomas myth through the Four Gospels
Know none are forgotten by the Creator's truth

Honor Every Soul path in the SToryTellers Planet

Unexpected Mirrors

Unexpected mirrors, dreams and teachers
Reflections that jump out hidden features

Denial is usually first que
Of subjects' repression long overdue

Extreme emotion signals you in me
Violent anger kindles truth be free

As pictures illuminate light and sound
Teachers awaken brethren sky to ground

Ending karmic cycles tallied debtors
Quicken best community inventors

Let dreams reflect joys path that mirrors just
Laughter swells to expand heart between us

Vote Free

In tears she sat
Identity under hat

Hear this voice
Awake choice

Know me
Vote free

CHAPTER 2

Awaken Master Consciousness

The Three-Fold Flame meditation and clearing practice to assist awakening the master energy of the cosmic consciousness of creation. The similar meditations of many humble practices of many ascended masters have been taught through many religions of the world. Allah, Amaterasu-ōmikami, Buddha, Jesus Christ, Ganesh, Krishna, Mahatma Gandhi, Stephen Hawking, Mohammad, Mother Teresa, Moses, Muhammad, St. Germaine, Joseph Smith, and Nikola Tesla are just a few names of exalted legends, teachers and cultural folklore of a few religions of the world. The great teachers who have assisted the world to illuminate the creative consciousness that brought unity to the heart core path to enlightenment.

My goal with this section of the book is to bring the beloved truths from each religion that have brought many to a peaceful wholeness path and shaped the acceptance of my own personal path. Though no spiritual eclectic practices have been more beneficial than meditating and honoring the universe of creation within all that is and all that is not. The infinity of God is lovingly referred to as The Great Mystery by my teachers from our American Indian heritage and represented as a living consciousness or metamorphic energy by others. Many rituals of the worlds' religions focus on purification of ill deeds that are felt to be untoward the advancement of the soul path or bring harm to the environment. It is through practiced reverence for rituals that the soul may be awakened to the memory of its' inspired purpose to be love.

The metaphysical movement, traditional religions and science technology are bringing together some of the more beloved practices to unite by a web connection for the inbetweeners of spiritual eclecticism. Over two decades of my nursing practice was dedicated to holding peace and love for my patients leaving their physical vehicles. Fueled by the love of various practices, I felt blessed to assist souls in transition to another dimension. Fortunately, I learned early on that the language of love unconditional was the only vehicle to hold peace in a pure space for souls to heal prior to physical death.

As a special blessing, I was bathed in spiritual bliss from many enlightened souls who honored me with messages from their dimensional journey. At other times, the bliss of transition from peaceful souls was so uplifting I was unable to sleep for up to forty-six hours. Though sleep is very important to health, a mystery of energy surge before end of life may bit a bit of a spiritual bliss contagion to those sensitive to the gateway of the divine transitions. Some focus on the brain chemical changes known to yogi practitioners in nirvana that is prevalent with family surrounded loved ones as they depart our need for daily hugs.

'The Web That Has No Weaver' by Ted Kaptchuk, O.M.D. a favored book at the Academy of Oriental Medicine honoring Chinese medicine philosophy but in its' title spoke of the cosmic consciousness of divine creation. I will never forget the divided heart that sent me to study traditional Chinese medicine when my husband's health began to fail after an electrical injury and diabetic complications. The drive to understand his Hopi Indian practices and my disjointed religions, began to make sense as the Japanese Masunaga Shiatsu Hara spoke of primordial health. Shizuto Masunaga was the great teacher illuminated by my Master teacher Pamela Ferguson through the art of Zen Shiatsu and began to heal my divided heart. It is an age-old story that tragedy awakens the hearts and minds to their imbalances to renew a life path in alignment with oneness.

Through Zen Shiatsu, Pamela Ferguson taught the empowering source of the universe that flowed through every sentient being to promote balanced health. With the Usui Reiki practices; I had studied, this congealed into a practice that merged the Zenergetic Transformation energies I began to embody in all my spiritual health practices. My first teacher in Usui Reiki and intuitive counselor, brought back some of my past life memories in healing energetics during my first initiation ceremony. Though it took a traumatic brain injury (TBI) from a car accident to remember my life path to be love; I renewed the belief in the miracles of the living Great Mystery of God and the Cosmic Consciousness within each cell.

As I walked one day over the hidden cave on my family's' property, I was delighted by the winged mating dance of beautiful butterflies. Inspiration for the miracles of living come as we are in gratitude of The Great Mystery. Nature is a most beloved inspiration for many of our indigenous spiritual practices of cultures across time. The more I release the tie to chronological and cultural labels to inspirational events, the greater my enjoyment of the eternal infinity of the cosmic universe. Perhaps it is my belief in the eternalness of our being or my scientific views of RNA memory that bring me to blissful appreciations in this life. Whatever the inspirational source or belief that drives daily existence, honoring the process in unconditional love has brought the greatest joy.

Ascended masters, the connection to the cosmic Earth, trusted friends, family love; as well as, exalted artists were some of the greatest inspirations that brought my fragmented gray matter back into spiritual harmony. I challenged my claustrophobic blunt force injured mind to expand to the out of body experiences of my trauma during a few too many near death experiences. The details of my car accident and domestic violence are minor in comparison to the lessons learned. What awoke in the grief process of the old me as I strove to remember the feeling of connection to a single cosmic deity was something within that connected me to a vast universal mind of God just out of full recollection. The trembling Earth, solar winds and voices of present pasts swelled into a swirl of awakened lifetimes. 'How I Feel' by Wax Tailor on Tales of Forgotten Melodies is a beautiful song that reminds me of the connections to all our memories in this beautiful story teller planet that graciously houses each precious life.

I woke up today and felt the rain of the cosmic Christ Consciousness cleansing my soul in the most beautiful baptism of the Holy Spirit beaming through every imperfection, I am a lover of traditional Christian faith values of sacrifices in love and the healing arts of many religions I studied. I truly have been given the gift of grace of new life within one; already having known love from a beautiful family. The people that we meet in every life follow us with heart felt lessons if we are paying attention we will know their sweet messages and heal the agony of separation. The Holy Spirit has always been the greatest communicator between souls separated by false walls of ego creation, though we are dependent of devices the spirit of the universe is heard in the quiet moments. However, we must honor that the lower ego is what has kept us anchored to Earth long enough to awaken to our unified consciousness with God, The Great Mystery.

The dualistic paradigm on current Earth reality continues to challenge us to remember the oneness of creation. The divine spark that heralds a joy so deep that we remember it in our dreams and in love shared with others from the pulse of the living universe. Sharing the joy of union with all is the most precious gift of gratitude for another in your life. Finding a companion or partner in life is a driving force in human existence which never faulters even after we have fostered children who gift us with their love. The gift of life is ever present as we cherish everything that the mystery of the universe brings us to awaken the sweetness of being in our Gods' presence.

Whether we believe that evolutionary sciences created the galaxy with the synchronistic beauty of the big bang or the majesty of the seven-day creation texts, something drives us to continue our pursuit of perfect expression. As humans we seem to be most joyful when our creations live past their original inception. Watching someone else enjoy and revision our dreams draws us to unite in greater oneness. Being able to share our dreams of a galactic perception without the limitations of our singularity, is one the sweetest acts of trusted friends. Applying connecting rhythms of life paths can unfold visions of holy bliss uniting souls in a body experience. The divinely inspired group healings started at age sixteen where prayerful teenagers at church camp became the conduit of healing for a beautiful counselor healed from throat cancer to more scientifically understood methods from Reiki, Zen Shiatsu and other cyber link connected spiritual affiliations used in Quantum Zenergetics Ask-ewe Solutions.

The metamorphosis of biological evolution has been illuminated through the Fibonacci sacred geometry series through the science of many master teachers. During a transformational revelation and emotional crisis, I felt the presence of the divine creator as an intuitive spark of enlightenment difficult to maintain any length initially. I felt the voice of the universe presented to me as a dynamic energy of numerical value bringing individuation to each life being as a metamorphic divinity expression. I was never a math genius but felt that intuitive mathematics within our cells unlocks the awakening of our master consciousness connected to eternal life. Perhaps the programmable mitochondria within each cell will be known as the limitless perfection illuminating God source which brings a joyful life. And since I believe that lady luck is a bit of a math genius there should be at least seventy-two qualities to the qualities we may choose to embody with each conscious creation.

Evolutions toward oneness with eternal infinity, discovers the multidimensional aspects to the vast universe. It is elation to experience dimensions where the living cosmic Spirit resides to assist and nurture. If we only see love that is what we draw to ourselves. Being completely in balance with all our chakras is important to draw only that which is limitless. Oneness is the being aspect of love. Understand that love is a totality of self, devoid of personal gain over others. Observe with understanding the movement of eternity toward union with the Great Mystery and be mindful of that which we hope to see continually repeated in our lives. Feel a sense of love unconditional to challenge discernment of that which is untoward perfection.

Be mindful that survival as a species or energetic being requires integral mind of the universal laws of creation. The circle or infinity rhythms to expand the limitless perfection of life in beautifully repeating Fibonacci spiral for our continuously needed review of limitless perfections. Be one with the rhythms of nature and respect that love in action flows through all life. Know that the dross or aberrant creations will come but allow them to pass into the abyss. Let the creative spirit soar and enjoy the vast universe of like-minded beings in the physical, a true expression of the creation community.

As we are drawn to a community of unconditional love and serve humanity to assist to disentangle tragic cycles, we learn to thrive as human beings of peace. You may feel the dream state awaken your soul before your daily life allows you to remember your wholeness, but do not wait until death ends your breath to know your perfection in creation. When my memories reinvested me to complete the grief of my late husband's death deferred five years prior, I was reminded that he told me "I am not the first nor the last to have ever loved you so". Richard Linklater in 'Waking Life' and Carl Jung's' many dream interpreters and engineers like Paolo Coelho in the 'Alchemist' teach us the mutable lines between our fifth dimensional dreams and third dimensional created reality.

As we remember past dreams of lives sprinkled in our subconscious or supraconscious mind, we may be blessed with loves that keep drawing us back into the somatic experience. It may be in the sounds of a distant familiar song or the light in the eyes of someone you seem to know beyond control. The truth of who draws you near fuels you to sweet bliss. The mystery of hearts separated by time is the energy that keeps the dream of past lives dramatically awakening on this sweet Story Teller Planet. Reuniting in oneness reflects the hope of healing this dualistic expression of false ideas of separation from ecstasy in limitless perfection of creations intent to wholeness.

The Spiraling Odyssey is a tribute to the voice that calls the infinite connection line to redeem the path envisioned originally by the vision quest inspired poem by Skip in "What Is, Is". This poem was the inspiration to a story that helped me to heal an intersection of my American Indian tradition husband's belief system; inspired by a cinematic genius in "2001: A Space Odyssey" to his last film 'Eyes Wide Shut' known as Stanley Kubrick; though quite frankly I never got the mystique of the poly amorous story. The poem combines some pasteurized American Indian theorist with many spiritual philosophies studied by me as the "wanna-be' philosopher, as I was described by my late husband. Though as somewhat of a genetic anomalous multicultural descendant, I learned through hitch hiking in a sacred dream that knights may be disguised as a balding man with a great smile. Foretold by my late husband to bring love and compassionate care to our family after his departure from physical reality in his poem "What Is, Is" by Edgar Loyd (Skip) Castle, Jr. His Comanche and Hopi Indian traditions of vision quest gave him the beautiful message that he would marry a blue-eyed Cyndy but unfortunately leave to the "Beyond Beyond" between the graduation of his two children.

Spiraling Odyssey

Spiraling odyssey awaken dreamers
Cosmic neolith or sweet redeemer

Captive docent or freedom creator
Remembering planet storytellers

Free to be truth invective recanter
Slumbering ever now dreams remembered

Where three-fold flames renew past and present
Great Mystery transform miracles mint

Hear my call to hearts time separated
Now light odyssey renews twin soul flames

Denounce duality rejoice oneness
Heal wounds sentient created genus

Meet mirror self-reflected joy in you
Strength of heart trust now love, and light imbued

CHAPTER 3

Dream Traveling, Multidimensions and Time Traveling theories

Lucid dreaming, astral or quantum traveling within your own holographic mind may be all the dimensional time traveling we desire or need. Most of us have dreamed of traveling down an expected path to work or play only to wake up lying in bed. As we learn to imagine the process and remember our experience, we wonder less that Deja vu is one of our favorite words. Quantum physics has long taught us about the observer in the experiment that seems to have a holographic vibration of multiple possible universes depicted in popular culture art. A simple but powerful expression of this may be exhibited when a popular show begins to connect writers, actors and audience, now popularized in a comment written by Stan Lee in 'Dead Pool' as breaking the fourth wall.

The unity principle in its' purest form can be learned from emphatically or energetically walking a mile in your neighbor's shoes. So, when we observe cycles and movements of our fellow man on Earth, we begin to connect our stories that remember we have been every character. We may even be able to imagine how easy it is to dream travel initially because we desire to be any character we have an emotional attachment. As a traveling empath, I continually learn how lucid dreams can awaken conscious realities for study and ultimately manifest our dreams into waking reality. Afore mentioned is a vivid cinema of waking dream fusion with daily life manifestation is written and directed by Richard Linklater in 'Waking Life'. In my story lucid dreaming, astral time traveling, and post concussive states merged a functioning mental corpse into an awakened observer. When we learn to embrace the stories that matter in love and non-judgement, we may find how to travel a mile through many dimensional selves.

In my Tibetan Buddhist studies, releasing attachments to perceptions outside ourselves bring us to limitlessness and even the keys to quantum healing. Quantum Zenergetics consciousness brings us a view from our multidimensional selves to break free of duality and into cosmic unity consciousness. Perhaps unity may seem opposite of multidimensional but in fact it simply refers to a singularity principle of creation discovered by Stephen Hawking in 2008. I like to think my best self is a non-judgmental free-radical creative conscious Stephen Hawking paradigm solutionist. Finding yourself at a point between love, pain and bliss is a life awakening way to discover quantum consciousness. We can either be frightened aware at the illusory nature of reality or amazed at the free will creative nature of conscious reality as we perceive it. We vacillate between our narcissistic home constructs and our cellular magnificence only to wonder at the significance of our awakened corporeal existence. We are the micro and the macro awakening consciousness.

We are light and sound in flux with the infinity. Awaiting metamorphic expressions of enlightenment and sometimes numerical value of cosmic stardust embodied within a vessel. We may even affirm as a conscious creator to transcend being any creative expression at any moment, the gleam of our conception within us. The concept of twin-flame, a buzz word out of popularity focused on missed opportunities of unions repeating in life cycles. We may now understand their sweet natures to create understanding of the metamorphic creations in the Great Mystery of God. Our life flames created by frictions of perceived imperfect love present a view of transformation energies well known by universal law expression to evolve to our highest intention in creation laws of the universe.

Being brought up for a time in the protestant religion, gave me the beautiful ceremony of water baptism. As with many traditional religions, an immersing under water with affirming prayers accompany the ritual. Recently I was reminded of the beautiful image of golden light that greeted me on the wings of a dove coming down from heaven as I read about Nikola Tesla's love of doves. The light and peaceful dove sound was a special gift from the living spirit of the universe for a renewed belief in miracles. It was special to have this gift in this observance outside in the sun that bathed me and my friends in a special hue one summer day of my baptism in a swimming pool. Even though I have gone on to study many religions, I always retain that a living spirit unites. In its' singularity divine it imbues the seventy-two qualities of the Great Mystery of God taught in the Hebrew religion that is a communion with the living cosmic creative consciousness. When feeling distant from loved ones, I have but to imagine the wings of a dove and feel the love that unites hearts in spiritual integrity communion.

Quantum Zenergetics consciousness brings us a view from our multidimensional selves to break free of duality and into cosmic unity consciousness. Finding yourself at a point between love, pain and bliss is a life awakening way to awaken quantum consciousness. We can either be frightened aware at the illusory nature of reality or amazed at the free will creative nature of conscious reality as we perceive it. We vacillate between our narcissistic home constructs and our cellular magnificence only to wonder at the significance of our awakened corporeal existence. We are the micro and the macro awakening consciousness. (Excerpt zenergeticreiki.com: Cynthia K. Castle, RN hospice nurse over twenty years.)

Grief and Lucid Dreaming

With a bit of trepidation, I include this section on grief processing with a lucid dreaming technique, but I recommend the use of a grief support team, counselor and spiritual shaman or minister. My main reason for caution is sleep excess is an escapism that can lead to or a sign of severe depression. If bereavement depression is untreated, the bereaved can remain in a compartmentalized introverted world in their grief expression. Once you have kept your promise to call a friend or grief expert for over-all health review, then proceed with fun. Allow your grief to express itself, the defined stages of anger, denial, acceptance, bargaining and acceptance as all are significant and severely disobedient to the prescribed order in their text order format.

The fear of expressing grief is something that many don't talk about because it's not Emily Post etiquette to cry inconveniently, so we don't. I say see a Doula expert and let it roar, then dial it back for office meetings so you don't get fired. But when you find it sneaking into daily decisions inconveniently, perhaps a bit of lucid dreaming may be the cure you need to heal and enjoy a memory review. The anger we feel is mixed with the fear of our own mortality in grief, especially when the death was not pretty. Most deaths are not Hallmark pictures, but every hospice nurse likes to help to make that the goal whenever possible.

When we are elderly or infirmed, another's death may even appear in the form of our own practice run for death. Remembering the rule is non-judgment in grief and throw out all societal should dos. In the 'Tibetan Book of Living and Dying' by Sogyal Rinpoche, I was taught about the illusions of death in the quantum universe as we make our way toward the divine expression of all that is God. Allowing yourself to cherish memories may even assist with a journey of becoming as you offer daily prayers in honor and remembrance. Grace is a gift given in many forms that many feel as a greater acceptance of self or forgiveness of others when we connect with our spiritual master teacher.

The American Indian tradition hold dream spaces as sacred as do other cultures and religions. As a rule of thumb, it its recommended to align yourself with a belief system with your grounding technique to give you some framework in your lucid dreaming. Rather like having a rough draft for a theme paper. Setting a prayerful or meditative positive attitude is important especially if you are on prescribed medications that has unfamiliar side effects. When you set your framework and attitude your lucid states can loosen attachments to negative habits and expand your awareness to the loss paradigm to make you aware of illusions or fears.

Whether we see death as a doorway to heaven or to a multidimensional school of creation consciousness, we can know the love of an eternal flame or holy spirit being that has always been with us. Over the weeks, months and even years the messages subtle to pronounce will remind us that our love flame is not as far as the flesh conceives. If we are adept at connecting with other dimensional consciousness, we may need to exercise caution to remember to be present in the third dimension long enough to pay rent and eat. But since you have already promised to have a physician, counselor, shaman or minister in this process, they are reminding you of this for me.

Point blank, some people simply need reminding to be in the real world and not living in dreams with their decedent loved one. If lucid dreaming is used as an escape to "avoid depressive" symptoms like normal tears, then we need to call our support system immediately especially if we are unable to perform mundane tasks of eating or paying bills. When we use tools to improve our daily function, teeth brushing and paying bills then it's healthy. In the initial phases of the first two years after loss, mark your calendar for anniversaries and birthdays as important self-care-caution day. The body carries memories for seven or eight years according to Chinese Medicine theories and will react on these days even if we are trying to forget those special or painful days. Many Asian, Latin and Hebrew cultures celebrate the passing annually of a family member with special meals and family gatherings.

An anniversary can trigger a deeper healing crisis or dimensional expansion doorway opportunity. Be particularly mindful of dreams and activities during these special days with a journal or artform. Always remember the stages are suggestions that may overlap or undermine the progress of healing if unheeded through denial or bargaining. My own accidents were most definitely serially connected to my deep denial of the series of surgeries over a seven-year demise of my husband's health. I felt responsible for the inability of insurance non-coverage of new pain treatments for electrical injuries, that eventually lead me to study the energy meridian systems of Oriental medicine acupuncture studies.

Be gentle in your process with yourself and never let yourself feel alone without resources or too proud to accept help you feel undeserved. Use the dream states for healing with care for quality of health including hydration. Visit your family physician early within the first month of your bereavement process as you likely neglected yourself while your loved one declined.

CHAPTER 4

Three-Fold Flame Meditation

The master teachers and way-showers each have methods to release ego definition of past labels, that facilitate a spiritual awakening or healing. Meditation in various forms accompanies most practices usually preceded by a prayer or affirmation of intention. Utilizing a universal mind consciousness or preferred spiritual master can streamline initiation toward your own personal process of expression. Even the focus of meditation on stress relief that extend the energy of the breath pattern to facilitate warmth in the extremities will improve bio-immunity.

One of the great things I needed after my first of a series of concussive head traumas was to learn a stillness of the mind. Though I am still struggling with this issue, I am learning from master teachers from the past like Buddha and Jesus of Nazareth. But triumphs taught by some our great teachers of today who help us connect past into present triumphs like by Dr. Brian Weiss (10) and Eckhart Tolle (1.) have helped many to understand that spirituality assists with positive health outcomes and a resilience in overcoming obstacles that improve life quality. (8)

> "When you are fully present with everyone you meet, you relinquish the conceptual identity you made for them —your interpretation of who they are and what they did in the past — and are able to interact without the egoic movements of desire and fear. Attention, which is alert stillness, is the key." Quote by Eckhart Tolle from "Stillness Speaks". (1.)

The twelve ray qualities of visual light spectrum and associated tonal sounds expand the mind with song and mantras. (2.) For this meditation, we will focus on three rays with their associated qualities that is begun with a focus intention affirmation or prayer. To remove the ego of lower mind which is limited in singularity intention, use an affirmation or prayer that gives reverence to God or the collective consciousness of life. Use your greatest ideal of integrity intention design focus to balance the twelve energetic meridians as understood in Japanese Zen Shiatsu or Oriental medicine. (2, 3 & 4).

The masculine blue ray of divine will can assist in transformative action energy, to begin the focus of energy reception between heaven and Earth. The divine love pink ray focuses on the choice connection of incarnation on Earth with remembrance of creation intention. The golden ray Christ consciousness ray refers to the son/daughter principle of procreation or master creation focus from a cosmic consciousness perspective. The master teachers like Buddha or Jesus Christ of Nazareth emulate qualities of healing compassion. For a greater vision of qualities to emulate you may find using references from the Jewish Hebrew use of qualities of God. (3.) A more in-depth study of associated sounds may help to attune a personalized mantra that may precede or be in conjunction with your affirmation intention prayer.

As with most meditations find a comfortable place that gives you a sense of reverence when you begin your cleansing breaths. Be sure to refer to the prayer of reverence for life prior to and during your meditation. Choose a prayer that focuses on reverence of life integrity creations for your highest good. You may choose to use this representation below as a particularly reverent prayer meditation prior to sharing love with your quantum soul partner and eternal soul family. Though many affirmations may begin your meditation, below is a universal consciousness source reference prayer that I use:

Be One in Wholeness

Be one in wholeness with God the Great Mystery
God the Father and Mother of creation - Christ consciousness

May we hardly notice the things that appear less than
wholeness to the Divine Will of heaven
Let us rejoice in blissful awareness of the eternal perfection intention of our creation

Proclaim oneness with the universe, a family of be love now
May Divine Love flow throughout conscious creations

Mitakuye Oyasin'
"We are all relations"
Namaste'
Shalom
Amen

Visualize a beautiful star birth nebula infinite in power of creative fire of the Divine Will consciousness. As you begin to be connected to the perfect timelessness of creative forces within the star birth nebula bring the blue flame of Divine Will through your energetic chakras connecting you from star birth to earth incarnation. Release the dross from the energetic unconscious aberrant creations, to allow transformation into conscious creation's light and unconditional love. (2.)

Visualize this blue flame descending the left side of the body through each chakra clearing dross for truth of creative intention down to the core of the Earth creative fires. As the blue flame of Divine Will meets the core it begins to ascend as Divine Love pink flame up through the right side of the body to seal the cleared dross with love back up to the star birth nebula.

As the pink love flame crosses over the blue will in unity creation of the son/daughter Christ Conscious, it presents as an unconditional love gold flame. It descends in a cascading ribbon down the front side of the body illuminating to merge as beautiful rainbow effect of light and sound breath of life creation down through the body to the Earth core flame.

As the gold Christ Consciousness flame ascends the backside of the body it reaches the root chakra to begin a spiraling DNA helix rhythm that ascends the central nervous system to awaken dormant spiritual qualities. Trust that only qualities that are for the highest purpose shall be awakened. Creation consciousness may connect us to the qualities that sustain Earth reverence.

Envision the rainbow iridescence spiral upward to the lower primal brain clearing effect of incarnation life karma to bring into balance and illuminate the cerebral gray matter now connected in full conscious creative knowledge. The twelve energetic meridians understood in Chinese medicine are being balanced throughout in harmonic resonance. The thirteenth chakra represents your consciousness that never left the highest intention in eternal creation. In the universal mind perspective, only that which illuminates truth shall be sustained eternally.

As the luminous three-fold flame of creation conscious spirals up through the upper heavenly connection chakras the perpetual torus field encases the physical body between heaven and Earth. The torus sphere illuminates the atonement colors that reflect aspects of the Great Mystery of the Divine Will in action by the heavenly Father, Divine Love of the heavenly mother and limitless unconditional love compassion in creation of the son/daughter principle of the Christ Consciousness.

The torus sphere envelopes the soma (body) and is the energetic eternal consciousness that feeds life force through the chakras connected to Earth and back up through the solar vehicle to remember the perfect intention of creation by cosmic laws. Envision your conscious creations manifesting abundant health and vitality for your life purpose, as you radiate within your protective torus field of divine quality light energy. Continue to bathe in the reverence of all creative life in its eternal purpose as you regenerate in limitless physical perfection removing dis-ease memories.

Dedications: My Father Merle Nellos, a listening American Eagle mechanic keeping our Blue Angels in flight one engine at a time and my mother Laverne an intuitive non-judgmental listening artist. To my angelic messenger teachers: my Great Grandparents John Yancy and Artincy Richardson, my Godparents Will & Shirley Minderman and Tom & Marty Harper, who taught how to embody Christ consciousness teachings of heart and the compassion of Buddha in their daily lives. To my foster parents Tom and Jan Warner who shared an opening to eternal limitless blessing for family and spiritual teachers blessed to awaken understanding of the heart compassion for creation reverence.

References:

1. Eckhart Tolle quote excerpt from 'Stillness Speaks' http://www.inner-growth. info/power_of_now_tolle/eckhart_tolle_stillness_speaks.htm.

2. Meditation techniques with permission modified from teachings from 1992 class by Will and Shirley Minderman and recordings of "Limitless Physical Perfection" series.

3. The 72 Names of God Meditation. (Though complete in entirety through authorized Jewish teachers, a sample may be found on sites such as: http://www.rose-publishing.com/Assets/ClientPages/Echart_namesofgod.aspx?gclid=CKX605nstM4CFdgYgQodH4kEeA)

4. "Shiatsu Theory and Practice" by Carola Beresford-Cooke

5. Being love with non-judgmental compassion taught by my Great Grandmother Artincy Richardson and Tom & Marty Harper.

6. 'Mirrors of Time' by Dr. Brian Weiss - techniques of connecting our whole self with our past.

7. https://www.webpages.uidaho.edu/rrt_psyc504/readings/spirit%20wellbeing%20HIV.pdf

8. With the assistance of Google search and Wikipedia research is possible for the homebound person looking to become something with their resonant voice. https://www.wikipedia.org/

CHAPTER 5

Masters and Mentors of today

Maya Angelou is an inspirational teacher who recited her poems at the inaugurations of President William Clinton and for the United Nations as a teacher and awakened spiritual friend of many. She freed us with her words that rang open the cage of the mind from 'Caged Bird' and taught me how to fly again as me. She helped campaign for equality for all and followed the inspirational teachings and marches of our equality hero Martin Luther King. Oprah Winfrey was a friend to many who brought us so many teachers to our living room including the life celebration of Maya Angelou just months before her passing.

Some of my favorite teachers brought to my living room were Paolo Coelho, Eckhart Tolle, Gary Zukav and Dr. Brian Weiss that we first heard in our living rooms as a personal shares of mentor teachers that taught us to awaken master purpose to be the heart vessel that inspires love to overflow. Maya Angelou taught the uncaging of our souls trapped by illusions of mind just as a favored author of fiction Madeleine L' Engle awakened that 'we are the ones' to share the light of heart to heal our planet". I believe this sentiment inspired our forty third and forty fourth President Barack Obama's legacy and my favorite quotable proclamation; "we are the ones we have been waiting for"; we must be the change we seek in unconditional love and equality for all "humane" treatment of human beings and the care of Earth resources.

My desire is this part of the book of affirmations and poems that may trigger your own joyous or tragic memories but breathe through the pain to find the teacher in you. When we connect with our highest intention of creation; our higher self, we oversee the limitless views of the reality we live in. When you have life transitions trauma or loss of a loved one, poetry can be a very healing release that gives you a rhythm to recreate a healing story. I began writing stories and poetry as a free bird trapped in the foster system and continued to collect stories of mentors and artists who helped in difficult times to remind me that we are born free to be love unconditional.

'A Wrinkle in Time' triggers from my favored book shared in read-a-louds with my children a way to transform even the most difficult situations. The stories that inspired this poetry series is hope to birth the brighter outlook told by our story tellers that make our planet a more heavenly place. For me the best of us is the non-denominational spiritually of unconditional love termed GranDogma as the sacred celebrations of all cultural spiritual stories that brought me back on point after near-death experiences from traumatic head injuries.

Honor Creative Word to Love
Teachings of Maya Angelou

The songs of the heart can never be caged
With God's power speak in words that heal rage

Overcome hate with our sweet thoughts embrace
End strife, reach to encompass healing grace

Honor Gods' creation; defend freedom
Let all hearts sing, be one in this kingdom

Sweet lessons bring joy; be one in Zion
Be love's unconditional champion

Release that which binds to liberate love
End mourning, awake gentle spirit dove

Know your path as generous teacher
Bring harmony to thrive humble creatures

Be righteous thought to satisfy your soul
Be joy knowing clouds reflect a rainbow

Revised 04/26/2018 World Peace

Life Path Redeemed

Tesla freedom in living sparks lightning

Energy crystals ground heavens Earthlings

Once forever in flight now sweetly unite

Bringing Eden home to hearts lost in night

Masters of light and sound now awaken

Bring peace to meek faith thought lost; now quakin'

Bridge the in between above and below

Anchoring souls energized now to know

The fuel of life's' nameless Great Mystery

Sweetly whispers love to hearts living trees

Spreading enjoyment through roots Tara core

Healing waters flow from heavens' sky door

Indigo children brightly sing the dream

Uniting separate life paths redeemed

Vote Freedom's Voice

Empower the sacred village of peace, voice your vote
The privileged power of voice brings protection's moat

Humanitarian economy brings family choices that thrive
Working hearts together insures best health to gleam pride

Equality of genetic heritage with cultural freedom to choose
Withstand assault against persecuted humanity's truths

Connections embrace to honor the Planet StoryTellers
Advocate witness of peaceful paths blazed by humanity seers

Communication integrity shares to glide on light beams
Thriving creative hearts living for citizens dreams

American Citizen Version 2

Empower the sacred village of peace this vote
The privileged power of voice brings protection's moat

Humanitarian economy brings family choice to thrive
Working hearts together insured in health gleam pride

Equality of genetic heritage with cultural freedom to choose
Withstand assault against persecuted Constitution's truth

Communication integrity security glides on light beams
Delighting creative hearts living American dreams

#VotePeace
#HonorthePlanetStoryTellers
#MovingHumanityForward
#RememberSelma

Honored by the American Disabilities Act of 1990

Awaken Planet StoryTellers
Sacred Village Earth

Springs of consciousness budding anew
After slumber recessed morning kissed dew

Learning to speak aloud and feel words form
They waited in patience looking for norm

The dreams seemed more familiar than day
Memory awoke pieced to show the way

The path to soar continues to strengthen
Resilient resolves; never beaten

Life brings joy to view through innocent heart
And simple pleasures of breath, the new start

The first morning contemplated, it's me
Was Earth Day remembering love of trees

She heals through life gifts of ocean spray
Embracing us her children on Earth Day

Let us resolve with power of thunder
Put an end to creations of blunder

Honor Great Mystery's gift of Earth heart
Bringing peace to new life journeys embark

Earth Day 2016 let it be limitless love.

Seeds Prolific to Bring Back Eden

World uniting hearts and minds in Love

Sweet songs bring peace release of mourning dove

Firefly children delight now sweetness rules

Lion meets lamb grasses grow no cruel

As above so below infinity

Heart fires reflect halo mind trinity

Dimensions Great Mystery in kind

Softly flow peace divine to all mankind

Bring joy end wars now, end fear of lack

Grow seeds prolific to bring Eden back

Innocent remembrance once forgotten

Love light release dross renew thoughts rotten

Bring heavenly days to humane beings

Open illumine loves' bright peace meetings

Peace Dream

In the thunder clouds a beautiful soulful dawning,
Awaken morning to sweet sound, angels yawning

Reverberant glorious rain resonant though the hills,
Peace soothing the valley through earthen cave thrills.

Ideas marvel in sovereign torus field space
Expanding cognizant end to ignorance race

Imperceptible paper ownership limits creative right
Heal now monetized energetic exchange plight

Co-create in sacred dream spaces, dawn peace
In every awareness knowing a mission of release

Dream of peace trusted soul families
Affirm humane being, thrive planet peace

Sublime

Lightning memories

Their hearts opened time

Ancient rhythm sublime

Joy Meets Trust

Dawn truth of hearts to twine in flight to light
Past care of lost delight once missed, not quite

Compassion star now sweet with beats one heart
Tears drip, vessels bound full for thee to art

Come bliss to quench open, shielded chambers
Of heart once drowned to pain of cursed labor

End fears doubt bring relief transformed to hope
Right held life past, now claim wild horse's slope

Vaulted dreams grace these flames to heights untold
Awaken love to meld entranced, now bold

Care clings to breath in sync of dreams to come
Now splendid, vision clear as joy meets one

Honey meadows fragrant as sky gleams trust
Shimmer moon beams now bright reflect in us.

Teller's Shell

The shell was named after him that was mine
The voice that spoke despicably, never thine

Years passed and the memory that seemed lost
Became details of my life that had been tossed

Always knowing there was falsehood somewhere
In the compartments yet feeling he knew me there

When I realized seventeen played our life details
Like a wave entwining to drown my life' ails

They called it science interactive to remove traumas clear
Unknown that it would never stop until blood smeared

Memory recoiled into many story re-tellers viewport
Until every angle crushed possible smoke like Newport ®

When I had no more stories to tell they wanted my families
Traumas that hurled details from their birth to drama tease

I as a nobody was never interesting to protections' power
But one day realized his name would be difficult to devour

Though trauma brain rooms continued more to remember
Knowing that my soul is real, impossible to dismember

They will know me one day from here to eternity
Mirrors display wounded heart without discerning pity

Cynthia Kay Castle

Be Clear Consciousness

Everything we say with loving intention is a prayer to the creator

When we thank a living being we are thanking its' creation

When we love, we love with the cosmic conscious intention of our creation

Be open with your hearts to hear your mind weep messages to clear dross

Release dross to clear for reuse that's formerly of aberrant miscreation

Allow the metamorphic energies of creation to bring abundant life

Be clear in your choices to preserve the sanctity of your unions

Be love together in more ways than you can count

Be beautiful in all your creations

Be pure love and light conscious creator

Shalom
Namaste'
We are all relations
In Lak'ech Ala K'in
I am You & You Are Me
Amen

*

The Planet StoryTellers

'Arms Ache'

Arms ache to hold in reflect of open heart love's bloom.
'Till then words flow to express reverie's joy of dawn's bliss with you.

Though I wake every morn with simple heart smile
The physical form still apart of unknown length in miles

In dreams the words transform your shape outlined in dew,
As we travel each night to meet at the cerebral transfer pews

The heaven's hold the stars collide
Points of light and sound crossed on galactic tides

Where we become all that we are or ever have been
A millennial or a moment outside time knows no sin

Are we creating a path or remembering the one of immense
Learned cosmic law pleasures to again bring bliss intense?

Will the want of physical connection now subdue?
The eternal energy torus outside time with you?

Will the laws that prevent the linear time wormholes
Conscious collapse keeps the soul trajectory knowing where to go?

Be Embraced

Let your sweet color of light and sound expand
Bring fusion of your senses to explode heart to hand

Move your happy feet to rhythms of underground caves
Rush with courage to embrace yourself in love, be brave

Open fullness to the artistry of nature's beat from source of all
Kindred spirits create the movement of timely hallowed call

Let lightning sparks fuel connection above down to your toes
Connect; knowing peace, accepting ourselves heals strife of foes

Be you in all your energetic fusion of light and sound
Embrace with heart's beating planting peace on hallowed ground

The Planet SToryTellers

Beauty of Heart

Beauty of heart and mind
Gift of joy from God to mankind

Precious light being know strength
In love surrounding your life's length

Angels sing when you smile
And laugh in triumph each mile

Release past fears and tears
Open room for joy my dear

Be protected from heaven to Earth's fire core
Leave fear and sadness as your guardian angel's chore

This poem was originally created for my sister Julie Anne because she kept loving me when I lived with her and despite my teenage behavior honored me as her once nurturing big sister. We have a tradition of reading poems and affirmations in times of strength building that helps us to empathically interface the world we love unconditionally.

Be Joyful Creation

Be a beautiful heart of cosmic mind
Gift of joy from Creator to mankind

Precious creation knows infinite strength
Let love and light surround us all life's length

Release emotions to joy past tears' fear
Always clear to open room for joy dear

Hear angel messengers sing with each smile
Heartily laugh triumphant each toiled mile

End fear of lack; let inner lions roar
Protected by Heaven to Earth's fire core

Dedicated to Heavenly Days
Copyright Protected
The Planet SToryTellers
© Cynthia Kay Castle 2016

Be One in Wholeness

Be one in wholeness to the Great Mystery of God
Father and Mother in son/daughter Christ consciousness creation

May we hardly notice the things that appear less than
wholeness to the divine will of heaven
Let us rejoice in blissful awareness of the eternal perfect intention of our creation

Proclaim oneness of heart with the universe, to be love now.

We Are All Relations

Mitakuye Oyasin

Namaste'

Shalom

Amen

Be the Holy Shift of Divine Will
Affirmation

Heavenly Father of Divine Will in Action, thank you for the Great Mystery of abundant life creation thriving in a creative sacred village in every dimension.

Thank you for the infinite beauty of quantum light beings who live, work, play and create with each other reverently.

Thank you for the creative infinite joy which fuels every mitochondrial energy cell in limitless physical perfection.

Promote healing through grace understanding of reverence for life eternal in the temple of each conscious soul energy.

May the Mother Earth vessel of receptive Divine Love receive love with each Divine Will action in reverent creation throughout infinity.

May the son & daughter Master way-showers honor the Great Mystery of God,
Sacred Creation
awaken in each being as taught through the lives of Master teachers.

Bless the messages of truth, science and peace honored by the Dalai Lama, Jesus Christ of Nazareth, Gandhi, Mother Teresa, Moses, Siddhartha Gautama Buddha and the Great Mystery of God.

Mitakuye Oyasin
Namaste'
Shalom
So Be It
Amen, Amen, Amen, Amen

Dawns to Oblivion

May we expand joy on the voyage in universal mind

If there is discord may I stand in your perception of truth

And trust that you can stand in mine;
Bring expedient harmony

Awareness dawns to oblivion;
Heal our amnesic souls

Release attachment to pain and suffering

Be awakened empowerment that heals

Inspired new dawn: open shields

Feel the vibrance of the universe waiting to be canvas for your beautiful dreams

May love's sweet breath whisper the message you need to hear

"For if the first and last have come and gone,
The best you may never know"1.

Inspiration Reference:
1. What Is, Is by Song Dog Poet 1954-2006 https://docs.google.com/document/d/18hQ_BSW02BH8bgmTv0C6nO2njoLIoJddvB8S775nYM8/edit
2. "Oblivion" by Joseph Kosinski

Gallant Focus

I felt the rain open my soul to know love again
It started as a fissure opening to a resonant grin

The pleasure of you unexpected, drawing me near
I could not stop the love that opened with a tear

The emotions had been closed for so long; I was duality
Either off or on, as if in slumber replete to sensuality

Like a dream remembered as one covered from head to toe
I began to awaken awareness that had been numbed in woe

Often, I did shutter that chosen focus was just too far to recant
Awareness now if too close, I would've remained vacant

Once unlikely friend's recourse original thought with guided intention
Glee with heavenly spark as electrical awareness escapes detention

The lack of being within my body started too long ago in fear of loss
Heart song stronger present when knowing pain removed dross

We laugh now in remembrance, a seeming irreverent focus intrusion
Known now as illumined mirror self in love sweet to life inclusion

May reverence never fain importance of knowing one that needed
Know the gratitude of strength found on a difficult path receded

I am here feeling toes touching the floor
Deliverance that breath loss was not the exit door

Hold laughter to awaken attention
In focus once too distant; sweet present gallant mentioned

Revised/Edit copy 08/09/2016

Lightning Fox

Focused intent on truth through winds of war
Clear eyes of will reveal detriments' scar

Anarchy ends with solutions birth node
Quick of wit to reveal costly decode

Branded purchase that frequency bets steal
Features once focused inspire better deals

Direction streams broaden deceptions conceal
Lightning flashed in dreams that time now heals

Let passions redirect quicken fox lightning
Kiss open natures door reverse death's sting

Listening pulse awakens connection
End lies of defamation projections

Quality awaken editor's floor
Share healing heart stories on crossroads shore

The line from my private dream journal (Within-Without or cleverly known as 7-8 reality of Cynthia Kay) that created this poem as I began to separate my fractured mind into a working book that could help myself and others to heal after traumatic brain injury or PTSD flashback nightmares: "Was it the kiss of death that awoke her from the electrical storm or the nightmares that replayed in digital byt3s echoing in linear time attempts on the walls of the cerebral amphitheater, she once called the 'quadrasphere'?"

Vote Freedom

Empower the sacred village of peace this vote
The privileged power of voice brings protection's moat

Humanitarian economy brings family choice to thrive
Working hearts together insured in health gleam pride

Equality of genetic heritage with cultural freedom to choose
Withstand assault against persecuted Constitution's truth

Communication integrity security glides on light beams
Delighting creative hearts living the American dreams

#VotePeace

Copy in Google Docs 2016 protected in The Planet SToryTellers

Metamorphic Expressions

We are light and sound in flux with infinity
Awaiting metamorphic expressions of enlightenment,
The numeric value of cosmic stardust vessel embodiment

May the transcendent being of creation express the gleam of conception within us
Cosmic soul union opportunities repeating until sweet natures of light create
Metamorphic creator flames that transform energies in love of
Universal Law expression

Be One in Wholeness
10/21/2013
Revised 07/02/2015

Dedicated to Heavenly Days Recovery Sovereign Equal S4cr3dTorus Rights for every human being and my late foster sister Anita. The sacred torus with alpha numeric reference format refers to the body as we ascend into heaven at death. It is also the Zenergetic perfection of us that fuels the body we are connected to in this life time that is referred to our sacred temple as a gift of life. This prayer are the messages I began to hear as a memory of a beautiful foster sister named Anita that I lost at age eleven. Her messages taught to focus on the love of God for the world and to release hatred for those that persecute us. These messages are perhaps the reasons why I try to release the pain of loss of old self and to love freely those who watched in sadness the complications of my quadrasphere complications of the PTSD diagnosis disability. Only in unconditional love taught to us by Jesus Christ of Nazareth and Masters of compassion can we move forward to a renewal of life. Perhaps the frustration of prejudices of the day is the reason I refer to the humane beings as galactic beings rather than just using humans. Those of us that recognize that unconditional love, may be a being able to achieve galactic peace as we end pillage of resources and war.

Galactic Beings of Peace

Redeem souls, awaken forgiveness now
End generations' shame; End fear of lack

Release prisoners to productive love environments
End exploitation of innocence

Consolidate businesses to end wars
Heal positions to know cosmic heart of Earth

Awaken masters to become Conscious Creators
End karmic hoards, be aware loving observers

End stagnate hoarded waters, let Earth emotions flow
Bring sweetness soothing an enlightened glow

End tortured dimensions to understand Universal law
Expand healing awareness through light and sound

Cynthia Kay Castle

Rejoice Cosmic Consciousness
Connect indigenous beings to aware Earth

Galactic beings of love and light be peace now

In Lak'eck Ala K'in

Mitakaye Oyasin

Namaste'

Shalom

So Be It

Amen, Amen, Amen, Amen
Reflect Divine Peace
Affirmation

See references and or definitions as required.

Be Creative Consciousness

I reflect I AM creative Christ consciousness, one with the Divine Will of heaven.

Illuminating within every energetic mitochondria cell of my body is Divine Love.

The Holy Spirit communication between the mirror creations hear and speak joy.

My vision is empowered by love's compassion for the highest good of all concerned.

The songs of angels connect our hearts for peace on Earth this day.

We Are All Related

Mitakuye Oyasin

And So, it is

Namaste'

Shalom

Amen

Stars Collide

May we meet knowing Arch Angels release
To enjoyment unbounded life treatise

True magic connection shim alchemy
Conscious observer now one trinity

Where heart thought meets sound and light, aura's field
May we open to merge bliss void of shield

Each breath a knowing of presence now found
Creation complex lost in moment

Where corners of Earth find crystal solace
And stars collide in platinum chalice

We are respond able bound to love's light
Cantilevers heart, magnetics in flight

Free in enjoyment of life, free to be
Waking each unfettered dawn sweet in glee

The sacred village earth is made of human beings who understand that art heals hearts to create the beautiful galaxy displayed for our luminous pleasures.

Gleams Trust
Dedicated to sacred maps to vulnerable hearts.

Dawn truth of hearts to twine in flight to light
Past care of lost delight once missed, not quite

Compassion star now sweet with beats one heart
Tears drip vessels bound full for thee to art

Come bliss to quench open shielded chambers
Of heart once drowned to pain of sunk tabor

Claim doubt to fear relief transformed, now hope
Right held life past to claim wild horses slope

Vaulted dreams grace these flames to heights untold
Awaken love to meld entranced now bold

Care clings to breath in sync of dreams to come
Now splendid vision clear as joy meets one

Honey meadows fragrant as sky gleams trust
Shimmer moon beams now bright, reflect in us

For Giveness

Forgiven, for giving of self too soon
Relieving sadness open's love heart bloom

Grace ends past where I am resolution
Cleansing debate brings healing solution

Focus frame of nightmare's past empower
Forever strong mirror Bardo devour

Awaken reverence create for life breath
Know eternal self never ends with death

Souls who meet this path awards now embrace
Each memory shares special one's heart space

May this sweet mind balance with healed grace heart
Hold place for dance of peace life to restart

Capacity of Love

I first met love as a counseling voice
She spoke careful to hearts of little choice

From the womb I felt my mother's tears
As I looked behind to see my sister's fears

My heart learned will to blink open its' eyes
Gentle care of her ant bitten blue eyed cries

Five ached emptiness for grandmother's sounds
Squeaking comfort rocker knowing no bounds

Our parents too young, we became state wards
Escaped trash shores in fantasy made art

Eleven showed us how closed eyes could see
Kerosene chopped hair once blowing in trees

End of rage Anita's story free roamed
Laundry train's lottery brought me new home

God parents fostered heart spiritual glee
As my number came up to set me free

They taught nature versus nurture and math
Though guilt poured to those left by an angels' path

Make-yourself-a-nurse grew to remember
The space where once we three dodged his temper

Vows to wed to the end, a man gentle
Opened love capacity, coyote's call

Trickster teacher by decades awoke friend
In hope that blue eyes love could break a trend

We entrusted to Earth her sovereignty
Her name roots of ash tree strong, free to be

Joyous bellowed laughter brought a brother
He brings gold heart to end doubting mother

The family four crystalline voids fear
Blessed with love for Great Mystery's revered

Pounding hearts grew strong near Enchanted Rock
Comanche strength remembered fate's time clock

Retirement forced, he cherished to know youth
Bringing coyote's call to stories of truth

Humane being tales indigenous ways
Snake medicine's life hard but death sweet bay

His heart left us open ways to master
Blue eyes both neared too many disasters

While root ash free to be, engineered skill
Bringer of heart's golden made light his quill

Her strength from heart hugs brought memories near
Life family blooms grow to weddings dear

Renew life be free Great Mystery's youth
Know end of doubt to six direction's truth

Light wakes past and statistical future
Through traumas voided heart, love speaks nurture

Capacity forgiveness big banged heart
Be love truth to trust without head of smarts

Congealed through pain of lost labor's nurse bag
Moon song dog's poet awakens from rags

Four years of doubt brought directions to clear
While night terrors of separate self-fears

Wind talker brings sleeper self to waken
Grandmother blue eyes words heard; ends quaking

Emotion's age equaling memories
Herald a chance to be love's reverie

Earth Day

Life brings joy to view through innocent hearts
And simple pleasures of breath of new starts

The first morn I contemplated, it's me
Was Earth Day remembering love of trees

As the pieces came together so sweet
I felt Earth hugs remind never retreat

She heals through life gifts through ocean spray
Embracing us her children on Earth Day

Let us resolve with power of thunder
Put an end to creations of blunder

Honor Great Mystery's gift of Earth heart
Bringing peace to life, new journeys embark

Create Art Resourcefully, a gift I learned as I created trash art on the beach from age 11 to 15. We can do better with the mysteries on our journey that need limitlessness of our unity perspective.

We are Earth the Planet SToryTellers

EarthDay2017

Eternal Heart Sisters

We can be blessed with the birth of loving sisters in our cherished bloodlines,
Some of us find an eternal heart sister, along a path that began a new time

Both enjoying a fruitful career that needed a heart infusion
For me it foretold of hospice, for her is spoke of her teaching heart

Struggling in the competitive career that diminished successful mothers
As an impossible persona who secretly left herself behind or opened sorrows

The more we opened to the joys of teaching in nursing
the more our spirituality bloomed
In friendship and Christ Consciousness the universe of
possibilities that left the past limitations

We began to enjoy sharing the multidimensional eternal
self that loved knowing a longer path
Outside of time and definition of country the lives of
past began to shape in her grandchildren

For me it became a place where the limitlessness
possibilities would honor the storytellers
That would bring us to know the ones who have helped
bloom many shapes and relationships in our lives.

May we always see the eternal heart of ones who shapes us by unconditional love,
You have been a sister, a friend and sometimes a mother that defends.

May you be blessed through all the stories you share in love
And nourish by your unconditional loving heart.

Dedicated to my sisters by my choice who never forgot who I really am Chris,
Cheryl, Cynthia, Jeanette, Judi, Julie Anne, Kat, Laura Ann and Patty.

Eternal Now Anchor

When light and sound meet eternal anchor
Arching of past present futures may soar

Awakening memories twixt and tween
Lives past aligning forever Now's been

Threefold flames hold consciousness embrace mirth
Light memories forever love's rebirth

Boredom abated creating joy now
When light & sounds unites limitless bows

The homogenous amalgamated
Aware and bright walking never jaded

Forged fusion clouds, linear crystals make
Moving through time wormholes we snake

Magnetizing infinity we draw
Perfect limitlessness creator's awe

© 2018 Cynthia Kay Planet SToryTellers

Everything Is Beautiful
God the Infinite Great Mystery

Everything we say with loving intention is a prayer to God
When we thank someone, we are thanking God for creating them
When we love, we are love with the God that created us

Be open with your hearts to hear your mind weep messages
that clear the dross and release life back in all that is and is not.

Be clear in your choices to preserve the sanctity of your unions
Be love together in more ways than you can count
Everything is beautiful in love of God

Mitakuye Oyasin

Names may limit infinite expression, The Tao

Grace Under Pressure
"Working Tech of Parent"

The decade milestones tend to cause pressure
We begrudge some more; our inside-du jour (6.)

Working parents focus life moments sweet;
Video records first steps memory treats

Now our brain tech aided by connections
Void absence guilt with VR documentations

Grandparents may elevate our emotions
Rewind enjoyment with VR devotion

Memory decades never lost, by tech returned,
Parent smiles at spinach art once concerned

Stains of life enjoyed - media complete,
Life circle all first steps - never delete

Dedicated to working parent stories in the Planet SToryTellers
And Happy Birthdays.

Definitions: 6.

This page is dedicated to an inspiration from a song by Neil Young 'The Words Between Lines' that inspired me to remember words we forget. Perhaps many should stay lost and perhaps the reason for the parable biblical story in the Tower of Babble. Today in difficulty of forgetting anything in print, we may need reminding that the story speaks of a weapon of words that decimated a city and created the rift between humane beings long ago. Cynz3n

Gratitude of Creation

by Cynthia Kay Castle

Every blade of grass brings the Eden principle to Earth
with gratitude of its' creation in love

Mistakes allow the illumination of the healing grace of
Pure Consciousness to shine through every darkness

Joy forever this day as one being unified infinitely sweeter
than the last now moment in love of unity

Know the sweetness of waters that travels through the womb of Earth
that nourish creation to illuminate love in all beings

Release the enmeshment of duality and the false reality of separation from God,
the Great Mystery of life creation.

Revised 07/02/2015

Happy Father's Day 2017

A collection of maps to share with the right query,
May just further a less bumpy joyous journey

One day when a half century of roads compiled
Revealed blessings lit with two hearts of freedom's child

Their father; gave his Song Dog poet's: roads to avoid
With his trickster smirks of hawk's call warn cynical voids

Our daughter studied his maps on her collection's ceiling
Her engineer's mind crafted a well-planned route of being

Our son took the scenic route fueled by heart's plan
Working with a light to serve his sure hands

This the first Father's Day after both of our children grown,
Known in the arms of their life's mate, making maps of their own

Looking down on his family we know the peaceful Warrior,
Smiles that his life great for starting maps; now he the freeform Ferrier

The Comanche nomad warrior of peace is happiest
Spreading surefooted good Red road paths of sweet rain zest

Happy Father's Day
From Mom, Ashley Bree and Zerin Thomas
Skip Castle
The Song Dog, Poet
1954-2006
© 2017 Cynthia Kay Castle

Hearts Awaken

Awaken hearts with beats of sound and light
Remember intent to love, and ease fright

The consciousness that creates our path heals
End the dormant slumber ignorance steals

The fear we lose when our love dominates
Brings joy to once the secluded isolates

Creative life from nebula's star birth
Renew youth's fountain from heaven to Earth

Stand proxy for those disabled once strong
Brighten days of hardship sounding love's gong

Be the arm that reaches to end sad tears
The empowered heart light sending love near

Break barriers to discern judgments knife
Bring peace to Storyteller Earth; end strife

A Mother's Dream

Rejoice heaven's creation, now be love
Know limitless perfection of gentle dove

Absent wars as humane beings unite
Sweet embraced heart truth ends war; clears with light

Awaken doctrines to pure love oneness
Transform evil design, resolve transgress

May wombs of humane beings thrive in peace
Cold hearts of lion's strife now laced by fleece

Purified emotion waters heal Earth
Energetic integrity knows life worth

Honor Earth Mother in Remembrance of Innocence the
Heavenly Limitless Be Love Intention

Identity Reconciliation

Our ideals create perfect illusion
But pure love draws to fill its' solution

The haze of passions' hype may rule out slow
Steadfast awaken synesthesia glow

Hold open your heart for more truth strengthens
Those that grow haste weary, lose truth beacons

Be steadfast, know worthy identity
Glitter shine passed, reveals integrity

Let chambers swell in identity truth
Souls eternal strengthen in winds of rouse

Let it be love's unconditional call
Soul truth message sweet, rare makes you stand tall

Joy Manna

Every day begins with fresh manna dew
In gratitude I Am able to reflect a joyful attitude

The obstacles were just the guide posts
The strong words made me stand against ghosts

Being present and pregnant with possibilities
Gives me inner sight and hearing for delicacies

The hungry ghosts of false fears no longer take
They were me oblivious to a limitless energy lake

New doctrine Be Love Unconditional, in love we create
Unify in strength of divine intentions, never to deviate

Let the season of compassion reign this day
Bringing back our childhood dreams and heart to play

The Planet SToryTellers ®

Joy Meets Trust

Dawn truth of hearts to twine in flight to light
Past care of lost delight once missed, not quite

Compassion star now sweet with beats one heart
Tears drip, vessels bound full for thee to art

Come bliss to quench open, shielded chambers
Of heart once drowned to pain of cursed labor

End fears' doubt bring relief transformed to hope
Right held life past, now claim wild horse's slope

Vaulted dreams grace these flames to heights untold
Awaken love to meld entranced, now bold

Care clings to breath in sync of dreams to come
Now splendid, vision clear as joy meets one

Honey meadows fragrant as sky gleams trust
Shimmer moon beams now bright reflect in us.

Kaleidoscope Glide

Sound focused convex curves of emerald
Heart breath opened caves of secrets untold

Sacred geometry paradigms infinite
Forging now from canvas life path distant

Shall we proclaim vivid orchestra glide
Or hard reality crash kaleidoscope ride

Each view port gave empowerment visions
Jingles of scenes collapsing decisions

Is right action to void awakened bliss
Or fate understood as dreams chosen kiss

May past doubts fade into fortune caress
Embrace full joyful heart with woes dismissed

Life Paths Redeemed

Tesla freedom in living sparks lightning
Energy crystals ground heaven's Earthlings

Once forever in flight now sweetly unite
Bringing Eden home to hearts lost in night

Masters of light and sound now awaken
Bring peace to meek faith thought lost, now quaking

Bridge the in between above and below
Anchoring souls energized now to know

The fuel of life's' nameless Great Mystery
Sweetly whispers love to hearts living trees

Spreading enjoyment through roots Tara core
Healing waters flow from heavens' sky door

Indigo children brightly sing the dream
Uniting separate life paths redeemed

Nature Nurture's Love Enchant

World of cogs and chimes only note cash loss
Fairy realm miss soul eyes lightened dew emboss

A gold meadow gift held open the door
Apologies advanced cold years in store

Only the trees knew expiration slowed
Cleansed air their counts as if for their betrothed

A vacant place lost, now found with your eyes
Reflections sound of joy colored blue skies

Kinetic heart that feels, conjures magic
Invoked light wakes voids to end the tragic

The invisible lost are kept by trees branch
Heart's desire call, nature seeks to enchant

Respond Able Heroes

Biological fluids trapped as stagnant memory pooled frights
Disjointed awareness striving to arc electrical dendrites

What dawns to consciousness is violent creation
Lost chronicles of time collated, may void damnation

Only the brave conjoins cerebral quadrasphere seclusion
To awaken exiled introspective to social inclusion

Connection doorways bring memories soothing tone
Relinquish fears that separated soul from home

Judgement may damn in a moment of unconscious act
One knowing honored a path off course assists me back

#Constitutional #justice #RespondAbleHeroes being
Driven reconciliators; end tears fall, open healing

Aho Mitakuye Oyasin*
Reverence of Life

Evolution of species in reverence of Life
Commit to wholeness derived of generations that end strife

Intelligent cosmic consciousness observers be love
Bring peace to all human beings, end the mourning of gentle dove

May the master creators path awaken peace
Of eternal reverent life with balanced Zenergetic release

Bring the integrity of cosmic elemental creative design forces
Open the hearts closed by divisive doctrine separatist courses

Cling to eternal joy principle of cosmic laws
Knowing the perfect intended creation devoid of flaws

Humane hearts thrive together as awakened star light
Where healing angelic songs bring dimensions flight

Dedicated to reverence for healing dreams of the peacemaker path in Planet
SToryTellers: Earth of humane beings, honored by the Lakota Sioux people.

Aho Mitakuye Oyasin*
"We are all related"

Reference:
Zenergetic release to website link https://sites.google.com/site/zenergetictransformations/home
Definitions: combine *d1., 2.

Smiles Speak Joy

Let your smile speak joy in the names you give one another
In the low sounds know that which is dysrhythmic
to Earth making ways toward unity

Kiss with joy in your heart for the blessing you have been given.
For the awakening in our soul has been knowing your rhythm
May we express joy in all ways knowing heart truth

Transformation Station

At transformation station, you may want to linger
But it's one of God's places to rest from your labor

Don't stop to think, it's nothing you can solve
Feel the Earth and let the birthing evolve

Listen to that So Ham rhythm, you "gotta" breath right
Let the mind's eye glow full in your void with heaven's light

Let love's passion flame cauldron feel desire through the heart
Never fear how light crosses sound where you let life restart

Thank God for that Willow City way where I learned to sing
At transformation station light moves with the sunshine you bring

Willow City was a place I first found the silence of the mind away from the city and multiple pager or cell phones to hear crickets and ground squirrels calling for their mother. A special oak tree named Luna Fleur was three hundred years old and taught to merge with the universe to feel the love of breath of life exchange.

Passion

The moment I saw you my higher self-acknowledged
a passion of time spent another day

Then I knew not the source of this comfort or Why
The very thought of you makes me whole

Our coming together feeds our joys and heals our pains
We flow through each other to embrace our entire existence

Our souls comfort in their passion of love unconditional
Your love pulsating through your veins penetrates my soul

You are very being caressing my desires
Your masculine urgency releasing my feminine passion

Your touch the spark igniting my desires
Surging with your powerful breath on my neck

Feeding the crimson and gold flame pulsating within me
Your moist breath whispering its way over my body
Laden with peaks of desire

I become lost in the journey as you travel
Valleys whispering promises of conquered peaks

Within each whisper my peaks swell with
Explosive flames reaching out to be consumed
By the passionate traveler

How intoxicated the drink of his creation, the
Traveler yearns for his own rewards

Momentarily I awaken from the journey and realize
That the passion still burning has not consumed me

I feel your intensions swell against me as
Your caressing tongue shares your drink over my breasts
And lips- now aching once again for your touch

You tempt my pulsating walls with your organ now swollen in anticipation
Your biting hesitation – you withdraw

In turn you cool your fiery mouth;
Your smile still glistening of lavish drink

Sharing my nectar, you grasp my hips to meet the
Instrument that would reveal untold passion

Probing skillfully these inviting walls
Your instrument excites my every recess

I too am intoxicated by the wine you bring from my well
We dance to the rhythm of your pulsing music

Rebounding against one another until synchronized in
Musical flames

For a moment expanded by our physical pleasures
Our souls soar in rhythmic fusion above our passions spent bodies

In the expanded consciousness we remember the first kiss so deliberate
We realize God is the source of our passion

Withered folds now illuminate timelessly as our heavenly smiles
Gently meld our bodies in loving embrace

Each other as one in loving gratitude of life creation
Thank you, Great Mystery, for bringing the other sweet map
To souls entwined where light meets sound

Dedicated to the newness of map of hearts to heal the fourth world in bliss eternal.

Mitakuye Oyasin

March 23, 1984 When poetry reawakened as I prepared for new life.

References and study resource suggestions:

You may enjoy some of the direct quoted references and a few decades of study from book and or spiritual link sources. This list is by no means comprehensive as I studied over twenty years intermittently and including some of my eclectic religious cultural infusions into my awakening to wholeness Lakota Sioux, Hopi Native American beliefs, Hindu, Japanese Shinto, Muslin, Scientology, Muslim, multicultural Paganism primarily Arabic to Norse-Celtic and Wiccan religions.

1. Quantum Zenergetics ® formerly Zenergetic Reiki before my traumatic brain injury and near-death experiences. https://sites. google.com/s/1bd7THAOIAhr6t3veh GHTYi3qhST2nXa/ p/0B5oRiZNy6Vn1TWpuZW5ZTzJEMm8/edit

2. Carl Jung Synchronicity theories: https://www.youtube.com/watch?v=BX_nMwYa-nw&sns=em

3. Bible versions including King James, Good News, Revised Standard and Catholic. There is also many other related books and original texts from the Dead Sea Scrolls, those forgotten like the Four Gospels of Thomas. 'The Lost Years of Jesus', The Book of the Essenes that focused on the lost years of Jesus that the Bible leaves out from his youth to his ministry in miracles. 'Conversations with God' by Neale Donald Walsh is among too numerous to name list of divinely inspirational authors.

4. Gestalt Psychology: https://www.merriam-webster.com/dictionary/Gestalt%20 psychology

5. 'Hand of God' a series created by Ben Watkins where I first heard the term radical acceptance.

6. Tibetan Buddhism: The Tibetan Book of Living and Dying by Sogyal Rinpoche. Traditional Ryoho Reiki spiritualism training practices. The Teachings of the Dalai Lama as read through social media over the last 17 years or so.

7. The Catholic Rosary prayer traditions that inspire me includes that of the Fatima and nine consecutive days of prayer.

8. My original article link https://app.grammarly.com/ddocs/169653369

9. Universal Life Ministry course, https://www.themonastery.org/training

10. The history of Charles and Myrtle Fillmore founder of the Unity Church of its' offspring Church of Divine Sciences http://www.unity.org/about-us/history.

11. The Jewish and Kabbalah traditions of meditating on the qualities of God and beautifully chanting the 72 names of God, http://www.72namesofgod.net/

12. Church of Scientology online volunteer ministers course https://www.volunteerministers.org/ Taught me to look up the ancient definitions or root word origin, even though I don't speak that way.

13. Sovereign Eagle Communication life and death transition privacy issues. https://docs.google.com/document/d/1LpzTUFkRB07QpuExBQtDZgFosl2SroRms5XCltRH5OY/edit

14. Synesthesia Migraine case study. https://docs.google.com/document/d/17RO95RUUDP-sNJ1aHKFJ1yVEvxITMwINAF7TfQj6ck8/edit11

15. Poem Postings, possibly original sites posting on Word Press but unsure due to writing manually in my "Gold Book'.
    a. https://wordpress.com/post/zenergeticreiki.wordpress.com/138
    b. https://wordpress.com/post/zenergeticreiki.wordpress.com/125
    c. https://zenergeticreiki.wordpress.com/2013/12/26/gleams-trust-4/
    d. https://zenergeticreiki.wordpress.com/2014/07/01/galactic-beings-of-peace-affirmation/

16. Rabbit Vortex references:

17. Program "Through the Wormhole" narrated by Morgan Freeman. Episode aired 05/10/2017 on the Science Channel. Great program that I am going to watch more of.

18. Pineal Gland DMT: http://www.trinfinity8.com/pineal-gland-dmt-a-pathway-to-psychic-abilities/

19. Zenergetic Transformations: Dream Vortexes and kaleidoscope healing paradigms https://sites.google.com/s/1bd7THAOIAhr6t3veh_GHTYi3qhST2nXa/p/0B5oRiZNy6Vn1TWpuZW5ZTzJEMm8/edit

References to awakening consciousness section:

1. Reference link to the pop culture genius of Stan Lee writer into his virtual cinematic paradigm proves to break the fourth dimensional wall of dream time to daily reality with his own brand of creativity to engage his adoring fans. The original Dead Pool referred to this in a big way. http://www.radiotimes.com/news/2016-02-18/the-9-best-superhero-in-jokes-and-easter-eggs-in-deadpool/

2. 'Waking Life' written and directed by Richard Linklater 2001 https://www.imdb.com/title/tt0243017/

3. https://sites.google.com/site/zenergetictransformations/hospice-concierge-service

4. Mixed diagnoses and grief: https://sites.google.com/site/zenergetictransformations/hospice-concierge-service/helpwithgiftedchildrenbycynthiakaycastlern#

5. Bardo as defined in books like: "The Tibetan Book of Living and Dying" by Sogyal Rinpoche http://www.goodreads.com/work/quotes/2899219-the-tibetan-book-of-living-and-dying

6. My website is still in transfer progress due to my disability vocational solution with the courtesy of Google sites who have fostered my site since 2011 when I first posted the use of my Zenergetic Reiki technique services. https://sites.google.com/site/zenergetictransformations/about-us

Cynz3n Definitions of multicultural, urban dictionary, pop culture or cynz3n version as required or understood in the waking of my quadrasphere ability to oneness communication ability.

1. Aho - "Aho" (あほ, アホ, 阿呆), a phrase in the <u>Kansai dialect</u> of Japanese, meaning idiot link reference: https://en.wikipedia.org/wiki/Aho

2. "Beyond Beyond" refers to the definition given verbally by many American Indian teachers that refers to a heavenly place like the Biblical definition of Eden on Earth. Where there are no wars, famine or property disputes in honor of the Great Mystery and the creator of limitlessness in the perfection of life existence.

3. **In Lak'ech Ala K'in - the Living Code of the Heart**
www.alunajoy.com/2007nov.html "In Mayan tradition, there is a greeting that many people working with Mayan wisdom know of. It is the law of In Lak'ech Ala K'in, which means I am another yourself (A modern day interpretation).

4. *"Mitákuye Oyás'iŋ (All Are Related) is a phrase from the Lakota language. It reflects the world view of interconnectedness held by the Lakota people of North America. This concept and phrase are expressed in many Yankton Sioux prayers, as well as by ceremonial people in other Lakota communities."* <u>*https://en.wikipedia.org/wiki/Mitakuye_Oyasin*</u>

5. *Ewe a noun inspired by a revision of lamb of God reference from Christianity that in Cynz3nism refers to a conscious creation solutionist who listens with unconditional love toward a vision of peaceful solutions. A Eweniverse in my 13 Monad theory is the ultimate personal vision of the divine intention of our creation as my gray matter conceives.*

6. Three-Fold-Flame Meditation created by Cynthia Kay Castle, RN Zen Shiatsu Practitioner 2004 and Reiki Master since 1999 with the angelic teachings by my adopted God Mother Shirley Minderman in 2005.

7. Giveness- Forgiveness versus for 'giveness" has a more that a few controversial reference viewpoints forming some of the divisive and opportunistic views of turn the other cheek and forgiving a debtor or transgressor. It should never be a conversation that divides religious viewpoints or court decisions that defame or humiliate the scapegoat or victim (ewe).

8. Gotta- a south Texan euphemism meaning you must or you are not thinking properly. Also makes it easier to sing in a Texas Folk song.

9. Quadrasphere- refers to the four-day review of short to long term memory stored and re-collated every four days while in recovery from a prefrontal brain injury with lightning synesthesia migraines zip file reviews that I dynamically recreative solutions as I did as a triage nurse for home health hospice and palliative care pain management positions.

10. Inside-du jour- is a term that I contrived to define the euphemism and spiritual eclectic beliefs that fuels many of us depending on popular culture or the majority agenda at hand.

11. Just ask me in an email light12x12@gmail.com for other things that should be clear or explainable to those of us unfamiliar with the things in between words unprinted by master teachers.

12. Planet SToryTellers ® the planet of SToryTellers where light and sound meet in rebirth of humane beings.

13. Respond Able Heroes – are those able to respond to the needs and become the inspirations to courage without regard to repayment and the best of a good Samaritan.

14. Zenergetic)Transformations) release refers to a technique contrived through the combined teachings of Shirley Minderman Angelic channeled energetic teachings, Donald D. Bacon, M.D. meridian visions in allopathic pain treatment, Usui Ryoho Reiki, Matsunaga Zen Shiatsu, 22 years of allopathic and integrated hospice palliative care transitions which may be explained in my website link more at length in the web link and numerous integrated medical articles. https://sites.google.com/site/zenergetictransformations/home

Printed in the United States
By Bookmasters